THE D.O.N. MINDSET

Mastering Emotional Intelligence to Build an Unforgettable Life and Brand

Be Different. Stay Optimistic. Know You're Necessary.

Donyale "The Don" Nicola
The D.O.N. Global, LLC.

Published by The D.O.N. Global, LLC.
First Edition: 2026
ISBN: 979-8-9944014-7-7
Cover Design: The D.O.N. Creative Studio
Interior Layout: The D.O.N. Creative Studio

This book is a nonfiction work based on the author's experiences, research, and perspective.

Every effort has been made to ensure the accuracy of the information herein.

Dedication

This is for you.

I wrote this book for you, the one who keeps showing up—especially on the days you want to disappear.

The ones who led through pain, loved through uncertainty, and still chose to shine.

May you always remember:

For the ones told they were "too much."

Too ambitious.

You are not broken. You are built for this.

You are Different. Optimistic. Necessary.

Too emotional.

Too different.

— Donyale "The Don" Nicola

iii

Acknowledgments

I give thanks to every soul who dared to see me before the world did.

To my ancestors—your resilience flows through my blood and breath.

To my family—both chosen and biological—thank you for shaping me with every lesson, challenge, and moment of love.

To my son and grandchild: Your existence is my greatest inspiration. You are my legacy in motion.

To my mentors, clients, and students: Thank you for letting me teach, learn, unlearn, and grow alongside you. You've expanded me in ways this book could never fully express.

To the ones who doubted me: Your silence became my sanctuary. Your resistance became my ritual.

Thank you for being part of my training ground.

To the "different" ones reading this:

You are the new standard.

You are the switch.

Keep walking—you're not lost, you're leading.

And finally, to The D.O.N. within me:

Thank you for choosing truth over conformity, purpose over performance, and emotional sovereignty over societal safety.

I love you for who you are, not who they expected you to be.

We are not here to blend in. We are here to break through.

About the Author

The D.O.N.
Different. Optimistic. Necessary.

Donyale "The Don" Nicola is a mindset architect, emotional intelligence mentor, and multi- dimensional creative, and the visionary behind The D.O.N. Global—a movement dedicated to helping purpose-driven people master their uniqueness, lead with emotional depth, and build brands that don't beg for attention—they own it.

Born and raised in New York City, Donyale's life has been anything but ordinary. A former teen mom turned transformational guide, a poet turned global speaker, an empath turned entrepreneur—her story is a testimony to the power of becoming. Not in spite of pain, but because of it.

Donyale combines 20+ years of experience as a mental health professional, lifestyle expert, and branding mentor with her own deeply personal journey of emotional healing, artistic expression, and spiritual rebirth.

> **Donyale's mantra: "Your emotions are not liabilities—they are leadership tools."**

Donyale is also the host of The D.O.N. Life Podcast, a sonic sanctuary for deep thinkers, soulful rebels, and visionaries ready to rewrite the rules of business, branding, and becoming.

Her presence, like her brand, is unapologetic.

Her work doesn't just inform—it transforms. And her writing invites you not to simply read—but to remember who you really are:

Different. Optimistic. Necessary.

When she's not coaching visionary entrepreneurs, writing poetic fire, or designing soul-based digital products, Donyale can be found sitting near waterfalls, reading beneath sunlight, or wrapped in silk—recharging in her ritual of solitude and sensual stillness.

To embrace the extraordinary, one must first master the art of balance—
between reflection and action, optimism and reality,
and the mind and heart.

Contents

Foreword

The world has changed. Since 2020, we've faced pandemics, recessions, uncertainty, and scarcity. But here's the truth: greatness is never born in comfort—it's forged in the fire. The D.O.N. Mindset was created for this moment.

This isn't just a mindset. It's a movement. It's the call to be Different when the world wants you to conform. To stay Optimistic when fear and doubt cloud the horizon. To know you're Necessary— because your voice, your brand, your vision is exactly what the world needs right now.

If you're ready to rise above scarcity thinking, to build a life and brand that can't be ignored, then turn the page. Because the unforgettable begins here.

Introduction

"This book is a mirror and a map, reflecting what holds us back and revealing the path to what moves you forward."

What Is the D.O.N. Mindset?

Where Growth Mindset meets Emotional Intelligence and Spiritual Rizz.

The D.O.N. Mindset was never designed to fit in.

It was created to break the mold.

It is not just a way of thinking—it's a way of being.

A way of leading with emotion, not despite it.

A way of building from authenticity, not an algorithm.

A way of owning your presence, even when the world tells you to shrink it.

The D.O.N. Acronym

- **D – Different:** You were not born to conform. You were born to switch culture, question the status quo, and bring truth to tired systems.
- **O – Optimistic:** Not fake positivity. Radical belief in possibilities, even while holding your pain.
- **N – Necessary:** You are not extra. You are essential. There is a version of the future that doesn't happen without you.

The D.O.N. Mindset says:

"My difference is my design.

My optimism is my offering.

My necessity is non-negotiable."

What Makes It Different?

Unlike other mindset models that focus solely on productivity or performance, The D.O.N. Mindset integrates emotional intelligence, personal branding, resilience, and daily micro-mastery. It's not about thinking positively—it's about thinking clearly, feeling deeply, and responding wisely.

It doesn't just help you "get things done."

It helps you become someone you trust.

Who Is This Book For?

This book is for the sensitive leader, the bold introvert, the creative visionary, the reformer in the room who's tired of playing small. It's for the soul who knows deep down:

- "I am here for more."
- "I feel everything, and I'm still powerful."
- "I want to lead in a way that feels like me."

If you've ever been told you were too intense, too emotional, too optimistic, too honest, too much of anything—this book is your mirror and your manual.

What You'll Learn Inside:

This is not a book to passively read. It's a practice.
A toolset. A soul tune-up. A personal brand power-up.

You'll learn how to:

- Use your emotions as fuel instead of fear
- Build a brand that feels like your truth, not a template.
- Sell and lead from resonance, not resistance.
- Create habits that nourish your nervous system and elevate your identity

Each chapter includes:

- A powerful lesson rooted in the D.O.N. framework.
- A quote or mantra to anchor the mindset
- A real mini-story from my personal journey.
- Journal prompts to turn awareness into action.
- Optional audio companion scripts for practice in motion.

A Note from Donyale

I didn't write this book from a mountaintop.

I wrote it from the middle of my becoming.

From the stretch between being overlooked and being unforgettable.

From the space where tears, triumph, poetry, and purpose all lived in the same breath.

I wrote this book for you—

The version of you who's finally ready to stop shrinking for comfort and start rising for legacy.

You are not here to survive your difference.

You are here to own, shape, monetize, and move with it.

And ultimately—lead from it.

Let's begin.

D.O.N. Mindset Diagnostic

Discover Where You Are — and Who You're Becoming

Before you go further into your D.O.N. journey, take a moment to check in with yourself. This is not a test. It's a mirror.

This 2-minute quiz is designed to help you see:

- How do you process being different?
- How resilient is your optimism really?
- How much do you own, your necessity in the world?
- How emotionally attuned you are in high-stakes moments?

You can retake it monthly as a practice of self-awareness and growth tracking.

No shame. No ego. Just reflection.

Be honest, not idealized

Use the results as a guide, not a grade

Let this be a conversation with your truth

Your score is less about "success" and more about where you are emotionally and energetically— right now. Let's check in.

Are You Thinking Differently, Optimistically, and as if You're Necessary?

Takes 2 minutes. Be honest, not idealized.

Instructions: For each of the 12 statements, choose the number that best reflects your truth most of the time:

1 = Never | 2 = Sometimes | 3 = Often | 4 = Always

Part I: Different

1. I feel comfortable being misunderstood if I know I'm being authentic.
2. I see being "weird" or "uncommon" as a strength in my life and business.
3. I use my story or uniqueness as a core part of my personal brand.

Subtotal: _____ /12

Part II: Optimistic

4. I believe my past challenges have shaped me for something powerful.
5. I can imagine a better future even when my current situation feels uncertain.
6. I actively train my thoughts to see possibilities, not just problems.

Subtotal: _____ /12

Part III: Necessary

7. I believe my voice, ideas, or art are valuable in this world.
8. I take up space without apology in rooms, meetings, or marketing.
9. I see my presence as part of the solution, not just decoration.

Subtotal: _____ /12

Part IV: Emotional Intelligence in Action

10. I can name and manage my emotions under stress.

11. I'm aware of how my energy affects others in business and relationships.
12. I can pivot my emotional state using mantras, breathwork, or movement.

Subtotal: _____ /12

Scoring & Interpretation

- **0–18**
  Scarcity Mindset Alert: You're likely thinking small, self-doubting, or suppressing your difference. Start with compassion. Then build clarity.

- **19–30**
  Transitional Mindset: You're aware of your potential but not fully claiming your power. You may toggle between visibility and hiding, optimism and fear.

- **31–40**
  Emerging D.O.N.: You're stepping into your Different. Optimistic. Necessary. energy—but could benefit from daily practice and emotional tools.

- **41–48**
  You ARE The D.O.N.: You lead from self-trust, use emotion as a guide—not a weight—and your presence uplifts and transforms. Stay consistent.

Next Step Recommendations

- Start the 7-day Emotional Power Practice (see journal prompts)
- Download the D.O.N. Audio Companion to reset on the go
- Take the Monthly EI Self-Audit in your D.O.N. Practice Journal
- Build from your results: The D.O.N. Mindset isn't a personality. It's a practice.

CHAPTER 1
Embrace Your Difference
The Power of Individuality and
Authenticity in Personal Branding

Chapter Summary

In a world obsessed with trends, templates, and sameness, your difference isn't a flaw—it's the foundation of your emotional intelligence and personal brand. To be Different, Optimistic, and Necessary is to show up with clarity, self-awareness, and courage in a noisy world.

This chapter explores how your individuality, when paired with emotional intelligence, becomes your most valuable asset for standing out in your industry and maintaining your self-worth.

Key Lessons

- Personal branding begins with personal awareness. You must know who you are before the world can recognize your value.
- Your emotions are data, not distractions. Embrace them to reveal your most aligned path.
- Scarcity mindset says "fit in or fail." The D.O.N. mindset says "stand out and thrive."
- Authenticity is your brand strategy, not just your personality.
- Emotional intelligence transforms your difference into distinctiveness.

My Story – "The Birth Certificate"

I wasn't named on my birth certificate.

I didn't find out until I was sixteen, standing behind the counter at McDonald's in a stiff brown uniform.

Working four hours every day after school to feel independent.

The end of the week arrived; check-in hand.

That's when I saw it. That blank space.

And something in me cracked.

It haunted me for years.

That empty line made me feel

Unseen.

Unclaimed.

Put away in a box—

Like that piece of paper no one bothered to read when I was born.

Forgotten.

Like, I didn't quite belong.

Like maybe I wasn't real.

But pain, when you sit with it long enough,

Becomes something else.

It becomes a purpose.

At 46 years old, I claimed my name: Donyale.

A name I earned—

Through poverty.

Through poetry.

Through motherhood.

Through every single day, I kept going

When I could've disappeared.

That act of naming myself wasn't just a legal decision.

It was an act of emotional intelligence.

Of radical self-love.

I stopped asking the world to tell me who I was.

And I became:

The Don.

Different. Optimistic. Necessary.

D.O.N. Quote

"When you learn to lead with your difference, you stop begging to be seen—you start branding your soul."

Journal Prompts

- What parts of myself have I been muting to be more accepted?
- What makes me Different in a way that's powerful, not shameful?
- Where has my authenticity created the most profound connection with others?

- How can I make my inner world (emotions, ideas, beliefs) visible in my brand?
- Who benefits when I hide—and who suffers?

Mantra: I Am Different by Design

(Say this aloud or record in your voice for morning playback)

I am different by design.
I am optimistic on purpose.
I am necessary by destiny.
I am not here to shrink.
I am here to shine.
My voice is a brand.
My emotions are my compass.
I walk in truth. I lead with light.
I don't chase—I attract through alignment.
I am The D.O.N

Audio Companion Script Preview

Begin with gentle breathwork.
Inhale.
"I am not here to blend in…"
'Exhale.
"I am here to brand my truth."
Inhale.
"My emotions are not liabilities…"
Exhale.
"They are leaders of legacy."

[fade into ambient instrumental or custom frequency track]

CHAPTER 2

Optimism as a Superpower

How Optimism Fuels Resilience and Emotional Mastery

Chapter Summary

Optimism isn't just "positive thinking." It's the emotional intelligence skill of expecting better outcomes and preparing for real-life challenges. It's the resilient belief that something greater is always possible—even when circumstances say otherwise. In business, in branding, in healing—it is optimism that keeps you visionary, bold, and in motion.

Key Lessons

- Optimism is not denial—it's direction.
- Resilience is not about bouncing back; it's about bouncing forward with belief.
- Emotionally intelligent optimism acknowledges pain and still makes room for potential.
- Optimism creates creative momentum—your best ideas are born from hope.
- You don't have to feel optimistic to act optimistically. Action generates energy.

My Story – "A Flood, A Pitch, and a Promise"

I was supposed to pitch a new creative series at an event in downtown Manhattan.

The morning of, my ceiling leaked. Water was everywhere. My notes were soaked. My nerves were soaked.

I stood there barefoot in puddles—laughing. Because I heard the old version of me whisper, "Cancel it. No one's going to get it anyway."

But my D.O.N. mindset kicked in: Different. Optimistic. Necessary.

I threw on my backup outfit, rewrote my pitch on index cards, and walked in as if I were carrying the cure.

That pitch didn't just land. It launched a contract.

Optimism isn't about waiting for life to go smoothly. It's about choosing belief when life gets slippery.

D.O.N. Quote

"Optimism isn't pretending the storm doesn't exist—it's packing an umbrella and rehearsing your victory speech."

Emotional Mastery Techniques for Optimism

1. Name the Narrative – Write out the story your fear is telling you. Then rewrite it as if it ends in your favor.
2. Reframe the Obstacle – Turn "This is happening to me" into "This might be happening for me."
3. Energetic Anchoring – Create a 3-word anchor phrase (e.g., "Peace. Power. Progress.") and repeat it when your energy dips.
4. The 3x3 Rule – List 3 things that went right today, three people you impact, and three reasons to keep going.
5. Future Memory Visualization – Imagine one year from today, looking back at this hard moment. What did it teach you? How did you grow?

Journal Prompts

- When was a time I chose hope over quitting? What was the outcome?
- What would the optimistic version of me do next in this situation?
- How can I prepare for challenges without expecting defeat?
- Where am I confusing realism with pessimism?
- Who benefits from my belief in possibility?

Mantra: I Believe In Better

(Speak with intention—stand up if possible)

I believe in better.

Not perfect. Not painless.

Just better.

I believe in the rhythm of rising.

I believe in joy after jagged moments.

I believe in my ability to switch the mood,

reset the tone, and rewrite the outcome.

I believe that what I carry is needed.

I believe that I am called, even when I feel messy. My optimism is not a weakness.

My optimism is my strategy.

Audio Companion Script Preview

[Soft, ascending tone with ambient background]

"Breathe in.

You are the carrier of a future not yet seen.

Breathe out.

You don't need certainty—you need alignment."

(pause)

"Say: I believe in better. I act as if healing is inevitable.

I lead with light, even in the shadow."

[Cue to gentle music fade]

CHAPTER 3

Why You Are Necessary

Reclaiming Your "WHY" for Purpose, Power, and Personal Impact

Chapter Summary

You're not just here to take up space. You are here to create space—for transformation, truth, and for others to rise through your example. The Scarcity Mindset says, "You're replaceable." The D.O.N. Mindset says, "You are necessary by design." When you root into your "why," you unlock emotional intelligence at a soul level—making every decision, brand message, and business move more intentional and impactful.

Key Lessons

- Purpose isn't found, it's revealed through reflection and emotional clarity.
- Your "why" gives your life and brand spiritual durability.
- Necessity is not about being the best—it's about being the most aligned version of you.
- People don't connect to what you do. They connect to why you do it.
- Knowing why you're necessary protects you from emotional burnout, comparison, and imposter syndrome.

My Story – "A Stage and a Stutter"

When I was 12,
I finally found my voice—
To perform live.
To stand in the spotlight.
To become a poet and a rapper.
But almost overnight,
A slight stutter slipped in.
Uninvited.
Unexplained.
Unapologetic.

Teachers/Producers told me:

"Speak slower."

"Stop performing."

"Stick to what's safe."

But deep down, I felt...

Necessary.

Not in ego—But in energy.

I knew—

If I could find my rhythm,

Someone else might find their voice.

That stutter?

It became my spark.

That fear of speaking?

It became the fire behind The D.O.N. Life Podcast.

Because my "why" was never about being heard.

It was always about helping others feel seen.

And when your "why" is rooted in service—

Your difference becomes divine.

D.O.N. Quote

"You're not here to convince. You're here to confirm—what's already been stirring in others. That's what makes you necessary?"

Mission + Impact Mapping Exercise

Take 10 minutes to answer these honestly:

1. My emotional story shaped me when...
2. The transformation I most want to help others experience is...
3. If I were to disappear today, what problem would remain unsolved?
4. The moments people say 'thank you' to me are usually connected to...
5. I feel most alive when I'm...

Tip: Don't just map your mission—map how it makes people feel. Emotions have an impact.

Journal Prompts

- What false beliefs have I held about being "too much" or "not enough?"
- When have I fel"t irreplaceable—not in status, but in soul?
- How does my story, pain, and perspective make me necessary to someone else's healing or growth?
- Where do I confuse humility with invisibility?

Mantra: I Am Necessary by Design

(Stand in front of a mirror if possible—say slowly and with conviction)

I am not random.

I am not a placeholder.

I am a spark.

I am a bridge.

I am a necessary part of the equation.

My experiences made me, but my why guides me.

I am not for everyone—but I am for someone.

The world doesn't need more copies.

It needs me—whole, aware, activated.

I am Different. I am Optimistic.

I am Necessary.

Audio Companion Script Preview

(Background: deep tones, affirming cadence)

"Breathe into your belly. Now whisper... 'I am the answer I've been seeking.' Again...

'My existence is on purpose. My emotions are intelligent. My story is structured.'

This is not the moment to shrink.

This is the moment to remember:

You were never optional. You were always essential."

[Audio fades with soft heartbeat rhythm]

CHAPTER 4

A Path to Power

*Gateways to Self-Mastery
and Emotional Regulation*

Chapter Summary

Power isn't something you take. It's something you reclaim—when you learn to regulate your emotional responses instead of reacting to every disruption. This chapter unveils the emotional intelligence tools that help you master your mood and your movement in life and business.

Self-mastery isn't control—it's a connection to your highest self. Emotional regulation is how you lead yourself forward with clarity, even when chaos calls.

Key Lessons

- True power is rooted in emotional regulation, not reaction.
- Self-mastery is not perfection—it's consistency in alignment.
- Your ability to pause, reflect, and respond with intention is a super skill in business and relationships.
- Power flows where presence grows.
- You don't need to control everything—you need to manage your meaning.

My Story – "The Phone Call That Didn't Break Me"

A few years ago, I got a phone call that should've crushed me.

An opportunity I'd been counting on—publicly—was pulled. No explanation. Just, "We've decided to go in a different direction."

The old version of me would've spiraled: "What did I do wrong?" "Why does this always happen to me?"

But that day, I sat in silence. I let the emotion rise, and I didn't run from it. I breathed, I wrote in my journal, and I reminded myself: This is information, not identity.

That night, I re-pitched my idea—tweaked, stronger, and more aligned—and landed a better deal within two weeks.

Power is learning how to process emotion without becoming it.

D.O.N. Quote

"Emotional regulation is a spiritual strategy. It's how you hold power without holding grudges."

5 Gateways to Self-Mastery

1. The Pause Practice
   Master the 5-second space before you respond. Breathe. Ask: What outcome do I want?

2. Name It to Navigate It
   Use emotional language fluently. "I'm not just angry—I feel unacknowledged." Clarity sharpens power.

3. Embodied Emotion Release
   Dance. Cry. Walk. Shake. Release through movement so it doesn't get stored in your body.

4. Reframing Ritual
   Ask: Is this situation against or growing me? Reframing interrupts spirals.

5. Power Posture + Breath Reset
   Stand tall. Shoulders back. Breathe deep into your belly. The body informs the mind. The stance informs the soul.

Journal Prompts

- What's a recent moment I regret how I reacted emotionally?
- What would mastery have looked like?
- What situations or people tend to knock me out of alignment?
- What physical signals tell me I'm dysregulated?
- What would it look like to permit myself to feel without falling apart?

Mantra: I Am the Calm Within the Storm

(Repeat gently, one phrase per breath cycle)

I am calm.

I am the clarity.

I am the current.

I release what does not serve.

I reclaim what always was mine.

My power is not performance.

My peace is not passive.

I respond with purpose.

I am self-led.

I am emotionally intelligent.

I am The D.O.N.

Audio Companion Script Preview

(Slow rhythmic pacing with grounding frequency beneath)

"Breathe deep. You are not your trigger.

You are the choice after the trigger.

Sit with your emotions. They are not enemies—they are data.

When you feel the fire, don't flee.

Stand inside it with grace.

Say out loud: I move from power, not panic. I master myself first."

[End with chime or heartbeat fade]

CHAPTER 5

Power of Self-Awareness

Emotions. Decisions. Clarity.

Chapter Summary

Self-awareness is the root system of emotional intelligence. Without it, your emotions drive you in circles. With it, your feelings become a compass.

This chapter explores how tuning into your inner world sharpens your decision-making, enhances creativity, and cultivates clarity in every area of your life—from personal relationships to professional moves. Self-awareness isn't just "knowing yourself"—it's learning how to use your knowledge to build what you need.

Key Lessons

- Self-awareness is the gateway to intentional living.
- Your emotions aren't obstacles—they are indicators.
- When you know your patterns, you can change your path.
- Clarity creates velocity—especially in business decisions.
- Creativity thrives when your inner world is clean and conscious.

My Story – "The Mirror and the Microphone"

I once recorded a podcast episode I was sure would go viral. The topic? Red-hot. The energy? On fire. The outcome? Crickets.

My first instinct? "Maybe I'm not relevant anymore."

But instead of spiraling, I listened to myself, not to the metrics.

I realized the episode didn't feel true to my voice—it was trendy, but not transformational.

I wasn't aware that I had started to drift.

So I deleted the episode. Re-centered. Rewrote. And recorded something that brought me to tears.

That one? It reached more people in 24 hours than it had in the last five combined.

Self-awareness is the moment you choose truth over performance.

That's power.

D.O.N. Quote

"Self-awareness is how you stop performing and start aligning. You can't master what you won't admit."

Clarity Mapping: Awareness to Action

Use this reflection process weekly:

Triggered Emotion	What I Felt	What I Did	What I Needed Instead	How I Can Respond Next Time
Example: Rejected	Anger	Withdrew	Reassurance	Pause, affirm, stay open

Your emotional awareness builds your decision-making blueprint.

Journal Prompts

1. What emotions am I avoiding because they make me uncomfortable?
2. What decision have I been putting off due to fear of clarity?
3. When do I feel most "in my body" and aware of myself?
4. What truth am I resisting that could set me free?
5. What version of myself am I afraid to fully accept?

Mantra: I See Myself Clearly

(Use after meditation or before difficult conversations)

I see myself clearly.

I see beyond noise, numbers, and narratives.

I trust my inner knowing.

I respond with truth, not trauma.

I do not perform to be praised.

I do not shrink to be accepted.

I do not delay clarity to stay comfortable.

I am honest. I am present.
I am D.O.N.
And I know myself—well.

Audio Companion Script Preview

(Soft piano keys in the background. Slow and steady voice.)

"Close your eyes.
Place your hand on your chest.
Ask yourself: What am I really feeling?
Now ask: What is this feeling trying to teach me?
Pause.
Say out loud:
'I release confusion.
I receive clarity.
I return to me.'"

[Sound fades with steady heartbeat rhythm]

CHAPTER 6

Resilience in Business

How to Lead with Strength Through Uncertainty

Chapter Summary

Business isn't just about strategy—it's about stamina. Resilience keeps you building, branding, and believing when the metrics are low, the clients are quiet, or the future feels foggy.

The D.O.N. Mindset reframes business setbacks as emotional data points—not signs of failure, but signals for refinement. This chapter will teach you how to lead like a lighthouse—grounded in purpose, visible in storms, and unshakeable in your belief.

Key Lessons

- Resilience is the bridge between vision and victory.
- Emotionally intelligent entrepreneurs don't fear uncertainty—they prepare for it.
- Your business must be rooted in value, not validation.
- Flexibility is not failure. Adapting is a leadership skill.
- Your emotional stamina is your greatest business asset.

My Story – "The Empty Inbox and the Bigger Vision"

One summer, the inbox dried up.

No bookings. No inquiries. No momentum.

I started to panic. Then I stopped.

Instead of chasing, I checked in.

I revisited my "why," refreshed my brand story, and created content that felt sacred rather than salesy.

That pause didn't just restore me—it reconnected me to why I built this brand in the first place.

Two weeks later, the inbox lit up—not from ads, but from alignment.

Resilience isn't always pushing forward. Sometimes, it's the grace to pause with power.

D.O.N. Quote

"Resilience in business is not about running faster—it's about standing stronger in your truth when the world isn't watching."

The Resilience Flow Framework (The D.O.N. Method)

1. D – Drop the Drama
   Notice when you're turning a temporary setback into a permanent narrative. Name the moment—not the meaning.

2. O – Own the Lesson
   Every "no," delay, or dip asks: What am I being called to clarify or change?

3. N – Nurture the Vision
   Resilience isn't just reaction—it's proactive care. Journal, visualize, and recommit to the next version of your mission.

You're not here to survive in business. You're here to switch the standard.

Journal Prompts

1. What business challenge recently tested my emotional stamina?
2. How did I respond: reactively, or reflectively?
3. What internal stories am I telling myself when the results don't match the effort?
4. Where in my brand or message can I reconnect to purpose?
5. What am I learning about leadership through uncertainty?

Mantra: I Am Resilient by Nature, Not by Force

(Stand or sit in a power pose. Repeat slowly with breath.)

I lead with grace.

I build with grit.

I don't break—I bend.

I don't fold—I flow.

When the world feels uncertain,

I become more certain of my worth.

My brand is built on belief.

My business is rooted in purpose. I'm not just in business.

I am the business.

I am Different.

I am Optimistic.

I am Necessary.

Audio Companion Script Preview

(Motivational with subtle, pulsing beat and atmospheric background)

"Breathe.

Business is emotional.

Let that be your edge, not your excuse.

You were built for the dip.

You know how to pivot with purpose.

Say aloud:

'When the numbers slow down,

I show up anyway.

When the energy feels low,

I rise intentionally.

I do not outsource my power to performance.

I own my presence.

I trust the process.

I lead from within.'"

[Audio fades with heartbeat and soft bass drop]

CHAPTER 7

Emotional Check-In Activities

Emotional Tracking Templates for Clarity & Regulation

Chapter Summary

You can't master what you don't monitor. Emotional intelligence requires rhythm and reflection—not just in moments of crisis, but as part of your daily mindset maintenance. This chapter introduces simple, repeatable check-in exercises and tracking templates designed to help you observe without judgment, build clarity, and regulate emotions before they hijack your decision-making or relationships. Like physical fitness, emotional fitness is built through consistent reps—not rare breakthroughs.

Key Lessons

- Check-ins help separate reaction from reality.
- Emotional data is powerful when tracked, processed, and applied.
- The more consistent your awareness, the fewer emotional surprises you'll face.
- Emotions leave patterns. Tracking them reveals the path to a breakthrough.
- The goal isn't perfection. The goal is presence.

My Story – "Tracking My Triggers, Changing My Tempo"

There was a stretch where I kept snapping—at my team, my son, and even my barista.

I chalked it up to stress until I started tracking my moods.

I used a simple color-coded system—red for anxious, blue for calm, yellow for hopeful, gray for numb. A pattern emerged: Every time I skipped a movement, ignored rest, or overcommitted, I went red.

Just seeing that on paper gave me power. I didn't need to guess anymore.

Now? I track my emotions like my revenue. Because one feeds the other.

D.O.N. Quote

"Clarity isn't found in chaos. It's found in consistent check-ins with your emotional truth."

Emotional Check-In Templates

DAILY EMOTIONAL SNAPSHOT

Morning Mood	Midday Switch	Evening Mood	Triggers/Highlights	One Word to Describe the Day
Anxious	Calm	Drained	Client feedback, skipped lunch	Paced

Use emojis or 1–2 words to keep it quick. The key is consistency.

WEEKLY REFLECTION PROMPT

1. What emotional patterns repeated this week?
2. What actions helped regulate my energy?
3. When did I abandon myself emotionally?
4. What boundary did I honor?
5. What do I need more of next week: Rest? Support? Structure?

FEELING-TO-ACTION MAP

Feeling	Meaning Behind It	Healthy Response Option
Overwhelmed	I'm stretched too thin	Delegate 1 task. Take a walk.
Insecure	I'm unclear on my value.	Review wins. Re-read testimonials.
Angry	A boundary was crossed	Journal it. Voice-note it. Protect space.

Journal Prompts

1. What emotion have I been ignoring that's asking to be heard?
2. What emotion tends to appear most frequently before I self-sabotage?
3. What emotional state produces my best work?
4. What routines best support my emotional baseline?
5. How would it feel to treat my emotions as sacred messengers, not mood swings?

Mantra: I Track My Emotions to Trust Myself Deeply

(Use before journaling or after a tough emotional moment)

I observe without judgment.

I feel without fear.

I track without shame.

My emotions are not problems—they are signals.

My awareness is not weakness—it is wisdom.

Every feeling is a page in my power manual.

I read them clearly. I trust them fully.

I am emotionally fluent.

I am emotionally fit.

I am Different. Optimistic. Necessary.

Audio Companion Script Preview

(Calm, minimal piano with ambient tones)

"Take a slow inhale.
Ask yourself:
What am I really feeling right now?
Don't fix it.
Don't explain it.
Just witness it.
Now ask:
What does this feeling want me to know?
Place your hand on your chest. Whisper:
'I am learning myself. I am not afraid of my feelings.
I am present. I am patient. I am powerful.'"

[Sound fades with heartbeat and wind chime]

CHAPTER 8

Emotional Intelligence and Sales

Resonating with Clients and Customers Authentically

Chapter Summary

Sales is not manipulation—it's a conversation of emotion and trust. When you sell from a place of emotional intelligence, you're not just offering a service or product; you're offering certainty, clarity, and connection. This chapter breaks down how emotionally intelligent entrepreneurs build client relationships that feel natural, necessary, and nourishing—because real sales begin with real resonance.

Key Lessons

- People buy based on emotion—then justify with logic.
- Your role is not to convince; it's to connect and clarify.
- Listening is a sales skill. Emotional cues are buying signals.
- Sales resistance often masks fear, confusion, or overwhelm—not rejection.
- The most profitable relationships are built on emotional resonance, not rehearsed scripts.

My Story – "The Client Who Cried in the Consult"

I once had a discovery call with a woman who barely spoke for the first 10 minutes.

I paused. I didn't push the pitch—I asked: "What made you reach out today?"

Her voice cracked. "I don't feel like I'm enough to do what I dream about."

Right then, I knew: I wasn't there to sell a service.

I was there to hold space.

I reminded her that her emotions weren't disqualifying—they were part of the brand. She didn't just hire me; she sent five referrals.

Because being seen sells, being understood retains.

Emotional intelligence closes clients without closing your heart.

"People don't invest in perfection. They invest in permission—to be seen, to be human, to be better. That's what real sales deliver."

EI Sales Framework: From Empathy to Enrollment

1. Ask for Emotion, Not Just Logistics
   "What's been the hardest part of this journey so far?"
   "How do you want to feel once this is solved?"

2. Mirror + Validate
   "I hear you. That makes total sense based on what you've experienced."
   (Validation disarms defensiveness.)

3. Switch the Focus from Fixing to Framing
   "What if this challenge is your next chapter's clarity?"
   Reframe their pain as purpose-driven data.

4. Offer With Alignment
   "Based on what you've shared, here's how I can support you."
   Make the offer feel like a bridge, not a bait.

5. Honor the Yes or No with Equal Energy
   Emotional mastery means detaching from the outcome and staying rooted in the impact.

Journal Prompts

1. How does my emotional presence switch when I'm in "selling mode" vs. "serving mode?"
2. When have I bought something based on how it made me feel, not just what it did?
3. What fear or assumption prevents me from fully showing up in my offers?

4. How can I use empathy to overcome objections rather than resorting to defensiveness?

Mantra: I Sell with Soul, I Connect with Truth

(Say this before calls, launches, or offers)

I do not chase.
I attract through clarity.
I don't sell to convince—I sell to serve.
My offers are aligned.
My energy is honest.
My presence is persuasive because it's real.
Sales is a connection.
Revenue is trust.
I am the brand.
I am the vibe.
I am The D.O.N.

Audio Companion Script Preview

(Upbeat but grounded—bass pulse with warm vocal tone)

"Take one deep breath.
Now ask: How do I want this client to feel after talking to me?
Not pressured, but powerful.
Not sold, but seen.
Say softly:
'I am not here to close deals. I am here to open transformation.'
This isn't selling. This is service, soul-led.
And I was built for this."

[Fade out with affirming tone]

CHAPTER 9

Marketing and Branding

Crafting an Authentic Message and
Relationship-Based Brand

Chapter Summary

Marketing is no longer about shouting louder—it's about showing up truer. Your brand is not just what you sell; it's how people feel when they experience your presence, your message, your mission. Emotional intelligence turns your marketing from a megaphone into a magnet. In this chapter, we explore how to create an emotionally resonant brand that builds authentic relationships—not just reach—and how to market in a way that feels powerful, personal, and profitable.

Key Lessons

- Your brand is an emotional ecosystem—it lives, breathes, and evolves.
- Marketing is about meaning, not manipulation.
- Consistency builds trust. Authenticity builds connection.
- People remember how you made them feel before they remember what you offered.
- Your message should reflect both your values and your vision—not just your value proposition.

My Story – "The Message That Wasn't Mine"

Early on, I followed a branding coach who told me to "sound more like the market."

I muted my voice, changed my tone, and made my content cleaner and safer.

The engagement went up.

But I felt off as if I were borrowing someone else's stage costume.

Then I posted something raw. My voice. My pain. My joy. My D.O.N.

It didn't go viral.

But someone DM'd me:

"You reminded me I'm not too much. I'm necessary."

That message? That's me?

That's the brand.

Authentic marketing doesn't chase applause. It creates alignment.

D.O.N. Quote

"Marketing isn't about being seen by everyone—it's about being felt by the right ones."

The D.O.N. Branding Compass

1. D – Different
   What emotional truth sets you apart?
   (e.g., "I blend strategy with soul.")

2. O – Optimistic
   What do you help people believe about themselves or their future?
   (e.g., "You can grow a business without losing your peace.")

3. N – Necessary
   What pain do you relieve or possibility do you unlock?
   (e.g., "I help you become who your clients are already waiting for.")

This compass guides your bio, pitch, website, and content.

Journal Prompts

1. What words or phrases represent the emotional frequency of my brand?
2. What emotions do I want my audience to feel after every post, email, or offer?
3. Where have I been marketing out of fear instead of alignment?
4. Who would still follow or buy from me if I never posted another "perfect" image again?
5. What part of my story deserves to be told more in my branding?

Mantra: My Brand is a Mirror of My Mission

(Say this before creating content or launching a campaign)

I market from meaning.
I brand with boldness.

My message is not borrowed—it's born.

I do not dilute to fit the feed.

I do not bend to trends.

I speak to the soul, not just the scroll.

I am Different in design,

Optimistic in vision,

Necessary by destiny.

I am The Brand.

I am The D.O.N.

Audio Companion Script Preview

(Confident, rhythmic tone with soft pulse and spoken word rhythm)

"Breathe deep.

Before you post. Before you pitch.

Ask: Is this me—or is this mimicry?

Is this aligned—or just approved?

Say softly:

'My voice is enough.

My vision is clear.

My brand is not a performance—it's my pulse.'

And those who are meant for it will feel it."

[End with a slow digital chime]

CHAPTER 10

How to Use Mantras to Reset and Refocus Your Emotional State During Challenging Times

Realignment Is Just One Word Away

Chapter Summary

Amid confusion, challenge, or emotional overload, your thoughts spiral—and your power scatters. This is where mantras become more than woo; they become emotional reset buttons. When repeated with intention, a mantra quiets the chaos and re-centers the soul. This chapter teaches you how to craft, customize, and use mantras to instantly reset your nervous system, reclaim clarity, and refocus your energy—especially when everything around you feels unsteady.

Key Lessons

- Mantras bypass the overthinking mind and speak directly to the emotional body.
- What you repeat, you eventually believe. What you believe, you become.
- Interrupting a negative thought loop with a mantra switches your chemistry and consciousness.
- The right mantra doesn't just motivate—it regulates.
- Mantras are how you "talk back" to fear, self-doubt, and scarcity in real-time.

My Story – "Mantra in the Mirror"

I once had a call scheduled with a potential investor. It was a big opportunity, but it also caused me a lot of anxiety.

My hands were sweating, my stomach in knots. I stood in front of the mirror and whispered:

"I am already enough. I am already chosen. I am already in the room."

I didn't say it once. I said it twelve times.

By the time I clicked "Join Meeting," my nervous system had caught up to my knowing.

I didn't show up seeking approval. I showed up anchored.

That call didn't just go well—I got the investment.

Not because I was perfect. But because I was present.

That's the power of a well-placed mantra: It puts you back in your body and back in your brilliance.

D.O.N. Quote

"Mantras are mindset CPR—quick, intentional, powerful. You don't need to be calm to say one. But you'll be calmer once you do."

The D.O.N. Mantra Method

1. Identify the Emotion
   Anxiety? Anger? Shame? Name it clearly—don't sugarcoat it.

2. Name the Need
   What is this emotion asking for? Reassurance? Boundaries? Confidence?

3. Craft the Counter-Mantra
   Build a phrase that speaks directly to that unmet emotional need.

Examples

Emotion	Need	D.O.N. Mantra
Overwhelm	Grounding	I breathe. I simplify. I move with ease.
Fear	Safety + Self-Belief	I am safe. I am capable. I am prepared.
Impostor Syndrome	Validation from within	I do not perform to be enough. I am enough.
Discouragement	Resilience	Delay is not denial. | I'm still the one.
Comparison	Self-Value	There is no competition for my assignment.

Journal Prompts

1. What recurring thought patterns challenge me the most during stressful times?
2. What do I most need to hear from myself when I feel off-center?
3. What old internal scripts (from family, culture, or industry) do I want to override with mantra work?
4. How do I physically respond after 3–5minutes of mantra repetition?
5. Which mantra will I commit to using this week—every morning and every moment I feel misaligned?

Featured Mantra: "I Am The D.O.N."

(To use when your energy is scattered, your confidence is shaken, or your emotions are activated.) I am grounded.

I am guided.

I am glowing.

My worth is not in what I do,

But in who I am—consistently.

I don't shrink to soothe others.

I don't hustle for belonging.

I move with certainty, even in storms.

I am not the product.

I am the power.

I am The D.O.N.

Audio Companion Script Preview

(Use a low, affirming tone with gentle binaural music or soft ambient loops)

"You are not behind. You are not broken.

You are becoming.

Say softly:

'I release the rush.

I choose rhythm.

I breathe in clarity.

I exhale control.'

You don't need to be fearless.

You only need to be faithful—to yourself."

[Audio ends with a heartbeat and subtle chime]

CHAPTER 11
A Collection of Mindset Affirmations to Boost Emotional Resilience and Confidence

Say it until you see it. Feel it until you become it.

Chapter Summary

Affirmations are more than cute quotes on Pinterest—they are energetic activators, emotional vitamins, and intentional declarations that switch identity from the inside out. When used daily, affirmations help rewire the nervous system, recalibrate the inner dialogue, and build a new emotional baseline of belief. This chapter delivers a curated collection of affirmations that support The D.O.N Mindset—Different, Optimistic, and Necessary is organized by emotional state, so readers can reach for precisely what they need.

Key Lessons

- What you say repeatedly, your brain begins to treat as fact.
- Your self-talk teaches your body how to feel.
- Affirmations are not denial—they are by design. They build the version of you you're choosing.
- You can't always control the thought—but you can choose the louder one.
- The D.O.N. Mindset speaks life, even when life speaks lack.

AFFIRMATIONS BY EMOTIONAL STATE

When You Feel Overwhelmed or Anxious:

- I do not have to do it all to be valuable.
- I choose peace over pressure.
- I breathe in clarity. I exhale chaos.
- I am not behind. I am right on divine time.
- I give myself permission to pause, reset, and rise.

When You Feel Insecure or Unseen:

- I am not here to prove—I am here to be.
- I am enough, even when no one is watching.
- I deserve to be chosen, even by myself.
- My light doesn't need permission to shine.

- I don't have to shrink to make others comfortable.

When You Need Motivation or Focus:

- My goals are not pressure—they are purpose.
- Every small step is sacred.
- I move with intention, not impulse.
- I do not chase energy—I create it.
- I was built for this. I rise by default.

When You're Healing or Navigating Change:

- I allow the old to fall away with grace.
- I am not lost—I am being rerouted.
- What's meant for me is magnetic and mine.
- I trust the rhythm of release and rise.
- Growth is not always loud. Sometimes it's gentle.

When You're Expanding in Business or Brand:

- My voice is valuable. My presence is power.
- Clients find me because I show up as me.
- I market from alignment, not anxiety.
- I am not the product—I am the pulse.
- My energy is the offer.

When You're Embodying the D.O.N. Mindset:

- I am different by design.
- I am optimistic on purpose.
- I am necessary by nature.
- My emotions are data, not drama.
- I show up as who I already am—not who I'm trying to be.

D.O.N. Quote

"Affirmations are soul rehearsals. Speak like the version of you who already knows you're enough."

Journal Prompts

1. What emotion or limiting belief is most dominant this season of my life?
2. Which affirmation feels uncomfortable—but also undeniable?
3. How does my energy switch after speaking life into myself?
4. Where in my day can I consistently affirm my identity and vision?
5. What three affirmations do I want to wake up to daily?

Mantra Stack: "I AM THE D.O.N."

(Use this when you need a complete energetic reset in 60 seconds)

I am grounded in grace.

I am guided by clarity.

I am guarded by truth.

I do not wait for confidence—I practice it.

I do not beg for belonging—I embody it.

I do not hustle for worth—I own it.

I am Different.

I am Optimistic.

I am Necessary.

I am D.O.N.

Audio Companion Script Preview

(Warm, spoken-word delivery with ambient piano or soft beat)

"This is your moment.

Not to perform. Not to perfect.

But to remember.

Say aloud:

I am here.

I am worthy.

I am necessary. My presence is a promise.

My light does not dim for fear.

I speak it until I believe it.
I believe it until I embody it.
I embody it until I become it."

[Fade out with rising hum and soft digital chime]

CHAPTER 12

Step-by-Step Guide on Incorporating Mindfulness into Your Daily Routine

Your Mindset Can't Grow Where Your Mind Is Never Present

Chapter Summary

Mindfulness is not a spa-day luxury—it's a daily leadership practice. Whether building a brand, running a business, or simply breathing through another busy day, mindfulness trains your brain to respond with clarity instead of chaos. In this chapter, we walk you through step-by-step how to integrate mindfulness into your morning, midday, and evening routines, so you're not just reacting— you're rooted. This is where emotional intelligence transitions from theory to lived experience.

Key Lessons

- Mindfulness isn't "emptying" the mind—it's noticing without judgment.
- You don't need 60 minutes—you need 60 seconds of pure presence.
- Small, repeated resets lead to massive mindset rewiring.
- Silence isn't the absence of action. It's the foundation of awareness.
- Every mindful moment trains your nervous system for leadership under pressure.

THE D.O.N. MINDFULNESS ROUTINE

Daily Schedule: Rooted. Real. Repeatable.

MORNING (7 Minutes): "SET THE FREQUENCY"

Step 1: Stillness + Breath (2 min)

Sit up. Place your hands on your lap or heart.
Breathe in for four counts, hold for 4, exhale for 6.
Say silently: "I am here. I am clear. I am grounded."

Step 2: Mirror Moment Mantra (2 min)

Look yourself in the eye and repeat:
"I don't chase alignment. I become it." Step 3: Mindful Movement (3 min) Slow stretching, shoulder rolls, or three grounding squats. Move with intention, not intensity.

MIDDAY (3–5 Minutes): "RESET THE PACE"

Step 1: Emotional Check-In (1 min)

Ask: What am I feeling right now? What do I need?
Write or voice-note the answer.

Step 2: 90-Second Breath Break

Inhale deeply 3 times while focusing on a single word (e.g., "clarity," "trust," "ease").

Step 3: Mantra Whisper Walk (1–2 min)

Stroll or sway while repeating: "I move at the speed of trust. I lead with grace."

EVENING (7–10 Minutes): "RELEASE + RESTORE"

Step 1: Body Scan Wind Down (3 min)

Lie down or sit back. Scan from your head to your toes and silently thank each part of your body for showing up today.

Step 2: Mind Dump + Gratitude (3–4 min) In a journal, list:

- 3 thoughts you want to let go of
- 3 moments you're grateful for
- 1 win, no matter how small

Step 3: Mantra for Rest (1–2 min)

Whisper or write:
"I've done enough. I am enough. I rest in worth."

Journal Prompts

1. What part of my day most needs a pause button?
2. How do I currently respond to tension—and how can I switch to presence instead?
3. What does "mindfulness" mean to me outside of apps or trends?

4. Where can I create a 3-minute margin to check in with my mind and body on a daily basis?
5. What emotion do I most avoid—and how can mindfulness help me witness it safely?

Mantra of the Moment: "My Presence Is My Power"

(Use anytime you feel scattered or stretched)

I slow down.
I listen inward.
I breathe on purpose.
I am not late.
I am not lost.
I am here.
My mind may wander, but my power is anchored.
I reset with breath.
I lead with awareness.
I am The D.O.N.—present, prepared, and powerful.

Audio Companion Script Preview

(Low hum, gentle wind, or heartbeat track behind voice)

"Close your eyes.
Let your shoulders fall.
Let your breath soften.
There is nothing to fix at the moment.
Nothing to prove.
Only you.
Present.
Worthy.
Ready.
Whisper:
'My mind is mine.

My focus is sacred.

My next move will be made in clarity.'"

[Fade with soft three-tone chime]

CHAPTER 13

Daily Habits and Routines That Support Emotional Intelligence and Personal Branding Success

Who you are in your routine is who you become in your results.

Chapter Summary

Habits are where intention meets consistency. You don't need more willpower—you need wiser patterns. Emotional intelligence and personal branding aren't about who you are once in a while, but who you become every day. This chapter guides you through building powerful daily routines that support your emotional state, sharpen your leadership identity, and reinforce your brand through aligned, repeatable actions.

Key Lessons

- Emotionally intelligent routines regulate your nervous system—not just your calendar.
- Small, consistent actions tell your identity who it's becoming.
- Habits are subconscious branding—your presence trains people how to trust you.
- Routine is not a restriction. It's infrastructure for creative freedom.
- The habits of The Don are structured in spirit, not suffocated by hustle.

D.O.N. POWER ROUTINES

Daily Habits to Anchor Emotional Intelligence + Amplify Your Brand

MORNING: Identity Activation (10–20 min)

- Mirror Mantra Practice (2 min)
  "I am not performing—I am presenting my truth."

- Feel & Focus Journal (5 min)
  What am I feeling? What do I want to feel?
  Who do I need to be to create that today?

- Brand Intention Check (3 min)
  One word I want to embody in every space I enter today:

- Silent Strategy Review (5–10 min)
  Glance at your plan. Breathe into it. Don't just do the day—meet it.

MIDDAY: Emotional Reset (5–10 min)

- Sensory Grounding Moment
  Light a candle. Play a calming sound. Stretch in silence.

- Affirmation Refresh
  "My voice is enough. My pace is sacred."

- Social Energy Audit
  Who or what drained you? What or who fueled you? Adjust accordingly.

EVENING: Reflection + Refinement (10–15 min)

- 3R Review: Recognize, Rewire, Reinforce
  What emotion led most of your day? Was it helpful? What will you choose tomorrow?

- Message Inventory
  Did my content, conversations, or decisions align with my brand values?

- Next-Day Emotional Forecast
  How do I want to feel when I wake up?

Prep one visual, mantra, or reminder that will cue that emotion first thing.

D.O.N. Quote

"Routines don't make you robotic. They make you reliable—to yourself, your vision, and your voice."

Journal Prompts

1. What do my current habits say about what I believe I'm worthy of?
2. Where do I lose emotional alignment in my day, and what could better anchor it?

3. What 3-minute ritual would switch my mood if I made it non-negotiable?
4. How does my personal routine reflect my professional brand?
5. What habit have I outgrown that no longer supports who I'm becoming?

Mantra: "My Routine Is My Reminder"

(Say this when you feel scattered, inconsistent, or emotionally reactive.)

My rhythm is sacred.

My habits are holy.

I do not need pressure to be powerful.

I do not need noise to feel worthy.

I move from devotion, not just discipline.

Each small act is a signal to my soul:

I am becoming.

I am consistent.

I am The D.O.N.

Audio Companion Script Preview

(Soft percussion or ticking clock rhythm—grounded tempo)

"Before you chase the next thing, return to the root.

Say aloud:

My habits hold my higher self. My routine is not punishment.

It's permission to show up fully.

I don't rise by force. I rise by flow.

My brand is not just seen.

It is felt through who I am, daily."

[Soft fade-out with heartbeat pulse]

CHAPTER 14

How to Build Emotional Resilience Through Consistent, Small Daily Actions

Significant breakthroughs are built on small emotional reps.

Chapter Summary

Emotional resilience isn't something you're born with—it's something you build. Not in one grand leap, but through small, daily acts of self-honor and emotional awareness. This chapter teaches how to strengthen your emotional core by taking consistent, low-effort, high-impact actions. These micro-habits stack over time to become the emotional armor and spiritual flexibility you need for business, branding, and life.

Key Lessons

- Consistency is louder than confidence.
- Micro-actions build macro-identity.
- Resilience isn't about being strong all the time—it's about knowing how to return to your strength every time.
- The brain rewires through repetition. Emotionally intelligent habits are neurological transformation tools.
- The D.O.N. doesn't push through pain—they practice presence through it.

5 Core Resilience-Building Actions (The D.O.N. Micro-Mastery Method)

1. Name It, Don't Numb It
   Every day, pause and name one emotion you're experiencing.
   Bonus: Rate it 1–10. Ask: What do I need to feel more grounded?

2. One Honest Statement a Day
   Tell the truth. To yourself, your audience, or a close connection.
   It could be:
   - "I don't know."
   - "I'm scared and showing up anyway."
   - "This no longer feels aligned."

3. **3-Minute Emotional Rehearsal**
    Imagine yourself confidently navigating something hard.
    Visualize it. Feel it. Hear yourself winning.
    Emotional rehearsal trains the nervous system to respond as if it's already happened.

4. **Practice 1 Boundaried "No" Per Day**
    Say no to something that drains you—even if it's a self-imposed should.
    One "no" a day reaffirms self-trust and resets emotional bandwidth.

5. **Daily 3–2–1 Reset**
    At the end of each day, reflect:
    *   3 things that grounded me today
    *   2 things I want to release
    *   1 thing I'll carry into tomorrow

    Write it, say it, or record it—witness yourself.

My Story – "The Day I Didn't Power Through"

I had a launch deadline.
A lump in my throat, tension in my chest, and my spirit saying, "Not today."
Old me? Push through. Perform. Pretend.
The D.O.N. in me paused.
I wrote in my journal:
"I am not available to emotionally hijack myself to look successful."
I walked. I breathed. I postponed.
The next day, I moved forward—not from pressure but power.
That's resilience. It doesn't always look heroic.
Sometimes it seems like honoring your humanity.

D.O.N. Quote

"Resilience is not about bouncing back—it's about returning to your truth faster each time."

Journal Prompts

1. What emotion do I struggle most to sit with—and how can I make space for it in smaller doses?
2. What small daily action helps me feel emotionally anchored, no matter what's going on externally?
3. Where have I mistaken emotional suppression for resilience?
4. What does resilience look like and sound like in my body?
5. What part of my current routine already supports my emotional strength?

Mantra: "I Practice My Power Daily"

(Use when you're tired, triggered, or tempted to revert to old patterns)

My strength is not accidental.
It is a decision—repeated.
I do not rely on mood.
I rely on movement.
One breath.
One boundary.
One belief at a time.
I do not chase resilience—I build it.
I am consistent.
I am courageous.
I am The D.O.N.

Audio Companion Script Preview

(Soft percussion with grounding string tones behind narration)

"You don't have to feel strong.
You only need to show up anyway." Say aloud:
I return to myself.
I return to clarity.
I return to center.

One moment at a time,

One decision at a time,

One day at a time.

Resilience is not my reaction—it is my rhythm."

[Close with quiet heartbeat or slow, confident footstep sound effect]

End-of-Chapter Reflection

You've just completed Chapter 14, but what you've really done is stepped into a new emotional operating system.

The D.O.N. Mindset is not something you visit occasionally.

It is a daily relationship.

It rewards attention. It thrives on presence.

You don't have to do it perfectly.

You only have to remember who you are—one habit at a time.

Closing & Tools

Afterword

The Becoming Never Ends

You are not a finished product—you are an unfolding power. This journey was never about fixing yourself.

It was about finding yourself in your feelings, focus, and frequency.

And now you know the truth:

You were never too emotional—you just weren't taught how to harness your emotions as data, direction, and divine design.

You were never too different—you were necessary to switch the narrative.

The D.O.N. Mindset is not a trend, tactic, or theory. It's a return to sovereignty.

A daily act of reclaiming your brilliance, not begging for belonging.

You've learned how to sit with yourself.

Speak life over yourself. Stand for yourself.

And serve from your overflow—not your exhaustion.

Whether you're building a brand, running a business, parenting, performing, healing, or simply choosing to keep going.

The D.O.N. in you is always present.

Not perfect.

Not without fear.

But rooted in the belief that your difference is your design, your optimism is your origin, and your necessity is non-negotiable.

This is not the end.

It's a reset.

An invitation to deepen the practice.

Because you don't become The D.O.N. once.

You are Different. Optimistic. Necessary daily.

D.O.N. Afterword Quote

"Your emotions are not obstacles. They are openings.

To deeper clarity. To a broader purpose.

To your next level.

Feel fully. Lead powerfully.

You are Different. Optimistic. Necessary.

You are The D.O.N."

The D.O.N. Practice Journal

Your Daily Companion for Emotional Intelligence, Self-Leadership, and Personal Branding

Daily Page Layout (One Per Day)

1. Today's Date: _____
2. Emotional Check-In

What emotions am I feeling right now?

- ☐ Calm
- ☐ Anxious
- ☐ Hopeful
- ☐ Frustrated
- ☐ Inspired
- ☐ Drained
- ☐ Energized
- ☐ Other: _____

Why do I feel this way?

_____

1. Daily D.O.N. Mantra

Choose or create a mantra to guide your emotional energy.

Example: "My difference is divine. My optimism is a shield. I am necessary in this moment."

Today's Mantra: _____

2. Intention for the Day

What emotion or mindset do I want to lead with today?

- ☐ Confidence
- ☐ Clarity
- ☐ Compassion
- ☐ Curiosity
- ☐ Focus
- ☐ Joy

My emotional goal for the day: _____

3. Brand Me Moment

What is one action I'll take today that aligns with who I am and how I want to be seen?

_____

_____

4. Sales or Creative Energy Log

How do I want to show up today when connecting with others? (Clients, audience, collaborators)

What emotional frequency will help me resonate today?

Example: "I will speak from warmth and clarity in my emails and calls."

_____

_____

5. End-of-Day Reflection:

What worked emotionally today? _____

_____

6. What triggered me or drained me?

My biggest emotional win today: _____

_____

One thing I'll do differently tomorrow: _____

_____

Repeat Daily — Make It a Ritual

You can print or duplicate this page for 7 days, 14 days, or 30 days to begin building a consistent habit of emotional clarity, mindfulness, and empowered self-branding.

Chapter-Based Emotional Companion Tracks

1. Embrace Your Difference (Chapter 1)
   The Mirror Mantra Reset
   Speak your truth while looking into your own eyes. A practice in reclaiming visibility and presence.

2. Optimism as a Superpower (Chapter 2)
   The Whisper Walk – Morning Edition
   Start your day with intentional breath, affirmation, and light. Best with nature or movement.

3. Why You Are Necessary (Chapter 3)
   Necessary in This Moment Meditation
   A short seated meditation to reconnect to your why—even when you feel unimportant.

4. A Path to Power (Chapter 4)
   The Regulation Ritual Includes breathwork, emotional naming, and a "switch the script" mindset prompt.

5. Power of Self-Awareness (Chapter 5)
   The EI Decision Download
   Tune into your body before making hard decisions. For clarity and grounded intuition.

Repetition + Reinforcement Tracks

6. Resilience Reset

   A 5-minute power loop for moments of stress, judgment, or rejection. Ideal before meetings.

7. Sales Energy Booster

   A pep-talk style mantra-based track to ground your value and align with a confident client energy.

8. Brand From Within

   Reminds you: you are the brand. Speak, post, pitch, and create from your emotional frequency.

9. Evening Release + Restore

   Let it go. Mantra + breath to clear the day and sleep with self-acceptance

Special Series: The D.O.N. Soundbites

- "You Are D.O.N." Confidence Loop
- "Different Is Divine" Self-Talk Reset
- "Pause Before You Post" Brand Alignment Prompt
- "Emotional Alchemy" – Turn Trigger into Power

How to Use These:

- Listen in the Morning While Journaling
- Pause Mid-Day for a Mindset Refresh
- Use Before a Pitch, Post or Difficult Conversation
- Listen on Repeat to Anchor your Transformation

Resources & Companion Tools

A curated vault for emotionally intelligent entrepreneurs and soulful brand leaders.

Audio Companion Series

Listen. Feel. Embody.

A collection of guided mantras, mini meditations, and D.O.N. mindset resets narrated by Donyale "The Don" Nicola. Perfect for:

- Morning Mindset Priming
- Emotional Resets Between Meetings
- Evening Reflection and Clarity

Includes:

- Mirror Mantra Reset
- The Whisper Walk Series
- EI Sales Energy Boost
- Confidence Before a Client Call
- Calm Before You Create

The D.O.N. Practice Journal

Pair this book with your own daily rituals using printable or digital pages that support:

- Emotional Check-Ins
- Daily Gratitude + Mood Tracker
- Affirmations & Mantra Practice
- Brand Clarity Prompts
- Sales Energy Log

Mini-Mastery Video Vault

Bite-sized trainings (under 10 minutes) designed to help you implement each chapter's lesson quickly.

- Emotional Intelligence & Selling Without the script
- Your Brand is a Feeling

- Emotional Forecasting for Business Clarity
- Building The D.O.N. Confidence Loop

The D.O.N. Assessment Quiz

Discover your current D.O.N. Mindset Alignment. Are you operating from difference, optimism, and necessity—or from scarcity and self-doubt?

- Get your custom profile
- Receive practice suggestions
- Track your growth

Monthly Mentor Memo

Receive curated guidance from Donyale directly to your inbox: affirmations, journal prompts, branding insight, and updates on live workshops and events.

Audio Companion Script Index

Emotional Intelligence on Demand
Each of the following guided audio experiences corresponds with the themes explored throughout this book.

Glossary of D.O.N. Emotional Terms (Expanded)

A reference for your emotional vocabulary as a Different, Optimistic, Necessary leader

The D.O.N. Mindset

A mindset rooted in self-awareness, emotional resilience, and authentic leadership. Based on the core belief that being different is a strength, optimism is a choice, and your presence is necessary.

Emotional Resilience

The capacity to feel deeply and still return to emotional regulation, clarity, and confidence. Built through consistent small acts—not big performances.

Emotional Check-In

A daily pause to name what you're feeling, what you need, and what would support your nervous system. One of the most underrated leadership tools.

Energetic Identity

The vibe your presence communicates without saying a word. Often shaped by emotion, intention, and nervous system regulation.

Mirror Moment

A practice of self-confrontation and affirmation. Looking yourself in the eye while declaring your truth, mantra, or intention.

Micro-Mastery

The daily 2–5 minute action that rewires identity. When done repeatedly, these tiny reps build emotional strength, brand clarity, and confidence.

Mantra Whisper Walk

An embodied form of meditation where you speak a calming phrase while walking. Used to regulate stress and switch focus.

Emotional Forecasting

The process of deciding how you want to feel in advance—and building routines or rituals to support that emotional state.

Pause Practice

The intentional act of not reacting immediately. Creates space between emotion and action. A core D.O.N. tool.

The D.O.N.

A self-leadership archetype. Not just a name—but a declaration of emotional power, brand clarity, and unapologetic truth.

To say "I am The D.O.N." is to say:
"I know who I am, I feel what I feel, and I lead with both."

www.ingramcontent.com/pod-product-compliance
Lightning Source LLC
Chambersburg PA
CBHW072147090426
42739CB00013B/3311